FIRST
BAKING
Activity
BOOK

HELEN DREW

DK

DK Publishing

Previously published as *My First Baking Book*

DK

LONDON, NEW YORK, MELBOURNE,
MUNICH, and DELHI

Art Editor Mathewson Bull
Photography Dave King
Senior Designer Neville Graham
Senior Editors Marie Greenwood,
Sue Nicholson
Production Amy Bennett

DK Delhi
Senior Editor Glenda Fernandes
Senior Designer Shefali Upadhyay
Designer Mini Dhawan
DTP Designer Sunil Sharma,
Balwant Singh, Harish Aggarwal

First American Edition published in 1991
under the title *My First Baking Book*
This edition published in the United States in 2007 by
DK Publishing
375 Hudson Street
New York, New York 10014

07 08 09 10 10 9 8 7 6 5 4 3 2 1
MD368 - 10/06

A catalog record for this book is available from the
Library of Congress.

ISBN 978-0-7566-2578-8

Reproduced by Media Development
and Printing Ltd, UK
Printed and bound by Leo Paper Products Ltd, China

**Discover more at
www.dk.com**

CONTENTS

BAKING BY PICTURES 4

PUFF PASTRY 6

PASTRIES ON PARADE 8

PASTRY IN A PAN 10

LIGHT AS AIR 12

CHOUX SHOW 14

SWEET AND SAVORY
SCONES 16

TEATIME TREATS 18

A RICH CHOCOLATE CAKE 34

DECORATED CAKES 36

HEALTHY MUFFINS 38

FRUITY BREAD 20

A HOLIDAY WREATH 22

PEANUT BUTTER
COOKIES 40

MAKING MERINGUES 24

SNOW-WHITE
SURPRISES 26

SIMPLE SHORTBREAD 42

COOKIE BAZAAR 44

LITTLE CUPCAKES 28

ICING THE CUPCAKES 30

FUNNY FACES 32

CHOCOLATE BROWNIES 46

A BROWNIE PACK 48

BAKING BY PICTURES

First Baking Activity Book shows you how to bake lots of delicious cakes and cookies. Each colorful recipe shows all the ingredients you will need. Step-by-step photographs and clear instructions tell you what to do, and at the end of each recipe are some great ideas for decorations. At the end of the book you'll find some tear-out stencil sheets. Use them to decorate delicious chocolate cakes (see pages 35 to 47).

How to use this book

How many cakes?
Each recipe tells you how many things the ingredients make. To make more, double or triple the quantities.

The ingredients
The ingredients you need for each recipe are shown clearly so you can see if you have the right amounts.

Cook's tools
These illustrated check lists show you all the cooking utensils you need to have before you start baking.

SWEET AND SAVOURY SCONES

Here you can find out how to make sweet scones, fruit scones, and cheese scones. The ingredients shown will make about ten scones. Below you can see how to make sweet, fruit, and cheese scone doughs. Turn the page to find out how to cut out and fill your scones.

You will need

120 ml (4 fl oz) milk

225 g (8 oz) self raising flour

25 g (1 oz) caster sugar

50 g (2 oz) sultanas

50 g (2 oz) grated cheddar cheese

50 g (2 oz) softened butter

A pinch of salt

COOK'S TOOLS

Baking tray *Wire rack* *Mixing bowl*
Whisk *6 cm biscuit cutters* *Measuring jug*
Rolling pin *Sharp knife* *Cheese grater*
Pastry brush *Wooden spoon*

MAKING SCONE DOUGH

Set the oven to 425°F/220°C/ Gas Mark 7. Put the flour and salt in the mixing bowl. Add the butter and cut it into pieces.

Rub the butter and flour together with your fingertips until the mixture looks like breadcrumbs. Stir in the sugar.

Add the milk to the mixture and stir everything together with the wooden spoon to make a smooth mixture.

Knead the mixture by pressing and squeezing it together with your hands until you have formed a stiff dough.

Fruit scones
Follow the recipe for sweet scones but add the sultanas to the mixture after you have stirred in the sugar.

Cheese scones
Follow the same recipe for sweet scones, but add the grated cheese instead of the caster sugar before you add the milk.

16

17

Cook's rules

- Only bake when there is an adult there to help you.
- Make sure you have everything you need before you start to bake.
- Always wash your hands, wear an apron, and roll up your sleeves before you start.
- Wear oven mitts when touching hot things and when putting things in the oven or taking them out.

- If you get burned, hold the burn under cold running water immediately and call for help.
- Never leave the kitchen when gas or electric burners are turned on.
- Always turn the oven off after you have finished baking.

Step-by-step
Step-by-step photographs and easy instructions to follow show you what to do at each stage of the recipe.

The oven mitt symbol
Whenever you see this symbol in a recipe, always put on oven mitts and ask an adult to help you.

The finished result
Pictures at the end of each recipe show what the baked and decorated cakes and cookies look like—scrumptious!

TEATIME TREATS

You can use different shaped biscuit cutters to make small scones, or make a big scone round with your hands. Scones taste best when warm, with or without butter. Try filling sweet or fruit scones with jam and whipped cream.

COOK'S TOOLS

Small bowl — *Whisk*

Sharp knife

Knife

You will need

Jam

150 ml (¼ pint) double cream

Sweet scones

Strawberry jam

Whipped cream

Cheese scones

CUTTING OUT THE SCONES

Grease a baking tray. Gently roll out the dough until it is 2 cm thick. Cut out shapes with biscuit cutters dipped in flour.

Put the scones on a baking tray*, brush them with milk and bake for 12 to 15 minutes, until firm and risen. Cool them on a wire rack.

A scone round

Whipping the cream

Roll the dough into a circle 2.5 cm thick. Divide the top into eight, then brush it with milk. Bake for about 25 minutes.

Whisk the cream in the small bowl until it is thick. Cut the sweet or fruit scones in half and fill them with jam and cream.

A fruit scone round

Grated cheddar cheese sprinkled on before baking

18

19

Sprinkle some extra grated cheese on top of the cheese scones.

PUFF PASTRY

You can make lots of mouthwatering pastries with ready-made puff pastry. Here you can find out how to make Eccles cakes, elephant ears, and cheese twists. The ingredients are enough to make about 30 pastries. Turn the page to see the finished results.

You will need

1 egg

¼ cup (50 g) raw sugar (for elephant ears)

½ teaspoon fine sugar (for Eccles cakes)

¼ teaspoon ground nutmeg (for Eccles cakes)

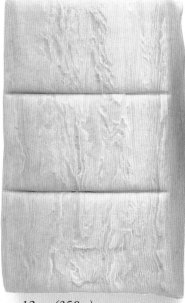

12 oz (350 g) ready-made puff pastry

1 Tbsp (15 g) soft butter (for Eccles cakes)

1 Tbsp (15 g) raw sugar (for Eccles cakes)

1 Tbsp (15 g) mixed zest (for Eccles cakes)

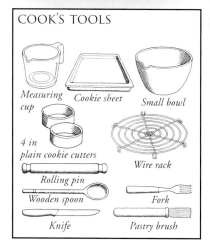

COOK'S TOOLS

Measuring cup   Cookie sheet   Small bowl

4 in plain cookie cutters

Wire rack

Rolling pin

Wooden spoon   Fork

Knife   Pastry brush

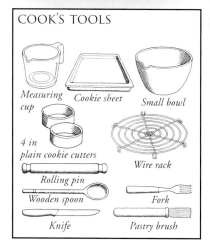

*2 Tbsp
(25 g)
chopped roasted
hazelnuts (for
elephant ears)*

WHAT TO DO

Set the oven to 425°F/220°C.
Grease a cookie sheet with some
butter. Beat the egg in a
measuring cup with a fork.

Put the pastry on a floured
surface and divide it into three
equal pieces. You will need one
piece of pastry for each recipe.

ECCLES CAKES

*½ cup
(50 g)
grated
cheddar
cheese (for
cheese twist)*

1. Roll out the pastry on a
floured surface until it is thin
and even. Cut out six circles
with the plain cookie cutter.

2. Put the currants, zest, butter,
1 Tbsp (15 g) raw sugar, and
nutmeg in a small bowl and mix
them together.

*¼ cup
(40 g)
currants
(for Eccles cakes)*

3. Put a teaspoon of mixture in
the center of each circle. Brush
the circle with egg and pinch
the edges together.

4. Turn the parcels over and
press them flat. Cut two slits in
the top. Brush them with egg
and sprinkle fine sugar on top.

7

PASTRIES ON PARADE
HAZELNUT ELEPHANT EARS

Roll the pastry into a rectangle 12 in by 8 in (30 cm by 20 cm). Brush it with egg and sprinkle on two-thirds of the sugar and nuts.

Fold the short sides of the rectangle into the middle. Brush them with egg and sprinkle with the rest of the sugar and nuts.

Fold the folded edges into the middle. Brush the top with egg. Fold the pastry in half to form a roll. Cut it into 16 slices.

CHEESE TWISTS

Roll out the pastry into a rectangle 10 in by 8 in (25 cm by 20 cm). Brush it with egg. Sprinkle cheese over half.

Fold the pastry over the cheese to make a sandwich and roll it flat. Trim the edges with a knife. Brush the sandwich with egg.

Cut the sandwich lengthwise into 20 strips. Twist each strip several times and press the ends on to the baking tray.

Baking the pastries
Bake the pastries on a greased cookie sheet. Cheese twists and elephant ears should be baked for 10 minutes and the Eccles cakes for 15 minutes. The pastries are ready when they are crisp and golden brown. Put the cooked pastries on a wire rack to cool. Pastries taste best on the day they are made, so you can eat them as soon as they are cool!

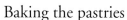

The finished pastries

Eccles cakes

Hazelnut elephant ears

Cheese twists

9

PASTRY IN A PAN

Choux (or cream-puff) pastry* is fun to make because it puffs up to two or three times its size when you bake it. Here and on the next five pages you can find out how to make and decorate lots of pastries. The ingredients shown below will make about five spiders, snakes, puffs, and éclairs, and lots of worms.

You will need

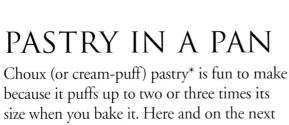

7 Tbsp (100 g) butter

¾ teaspoon salt

4 eggs

1 cup (150 g) flour

1 beaten egg

8 fl oz (250 ml) water

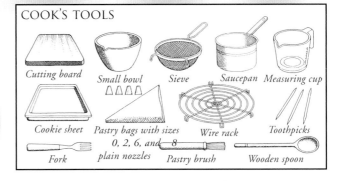

COOK'S TOOLS

Cutting board   *Small bowl*   *Sieve*   *Saucepan*   *Measuring cup*

Cookie sheet   *Pastry bags with sizes 0, 2, 6, and 8 plain nozzles*   *Wire rack*   *Toothpicks*

Fork   *Pastry brush*   *Wooden spoon*

10

Choux is French for puff.

WHAT TO DO

1. Set the oven to 400°F/200°C. Grease the cookie sheet. Sift the flour into the small bowl.

2. Put the water, salt, and butter into the pan and heat them gently until the butter has melted and the mixture begins to bubble.

3. Remove the saucepan from the heat and stand it on a cutting board. Add all the flour to the mixture all at once.

4. Beat the mixture vigorously until it comes away from the sides of the saucepan. Leave it to cool for one to two minutes.

5. Beat the eggs in the small bowl. Add them to the mixture a little at a time until it is smooth and shiny.

6. Fit a nozzle* into the pastry bag. Put the bag in the measuring cup and fold its top over the sides. Spoon in the mixture.

7. When the bag is full, twist the top to close it. To form the shapes, squeeze the pastry down through the nozzle.

8. Squeeze your shapes on to the cookie sheet and brush them with beaten egg. Bake them for 20 to 25 minutes until golden.

9. Remove the shapes from the oven and prick each one with a toothpick. Place the shapes on a wire rack to cool.

Turn the page to see which nozzle to use to form each shape.

LIGHT AS AIR

You can form choux pastry into any shape you like. Follow the instructions at the bottom of the page to make spiders, snakes, worms, puffs, and éclairs. When the shapes are cool, fill them with whipped cream and top them with the chocolate icing shown opposite.

You will need

1½ cups (100 g) powdered sugar

4 oz (100 g) chocolate

PUFFS

To make puffs and spiders' bodies, use the size 8 nozzle and form small, round piles on to the cookie sheet.

SNAKES

Use the size 6 nozzle to make the snakes. Start at the head of the snake and make a wiggly line for its body.

SPIDERS' LEGS

Form the spiders' legs with the size 0 nozzle. Make four left legs and four right legs for each spider.

WORMS

These are made with a size 2 nozzle. Form the worms as if you were writing commas.

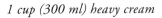

1 cup (300 ml) heavy cream

2 Tbsp (25 g) butter

3 tablespoons water

COOK'S TOOLS

Whisk   Sieve

2 small bowls

Wooden spoon

Spatula knife

ECLAIRS

Eclairs are made with the size 8 nozzle. Use 2 in (5 cm) lines of pastry for mini éclairs and 4 in (10 cm) lines for big ones.

WHAT TO DO

1. Whisk the cream in a small bowl until it is thick and fluffy. Slice the puffs and éclairs in half and spoon the cream into them.

2. Cut the butter and chocolate into pieces. Put them in the saucepan and stir them together over a low heat until they melt.

3. Stir in the water. Remove the mixture from the heat. Sift the powdered sugar and add it to the mixture. Stir until smooth.

4. Spread icing along the buns, éclairs, and snakes with a spatula knife. Dip the worms in the icing with your fingers.

13

CHOUX SHOW

Here are some ideas for decorating your choux shapes. The spider's web was made by piping some of the chocolate icing on to a large white plate. Try piping other animals to make a choux zoo for a special meal or party.

The finished shapes

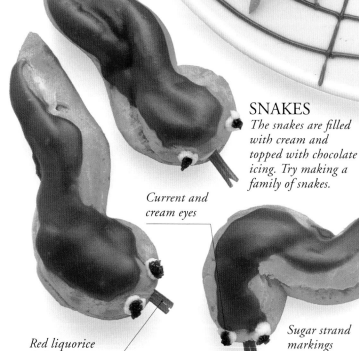

Currants

Red liquorice

Multicolored sprinkles

Sugar strands

SNAKES
The snakes are filled with cream and topped with chocolate icing. Try making a family of snakes.

Current and cream eyes

Red liquorice forked tongue

Sugar strand markings

14

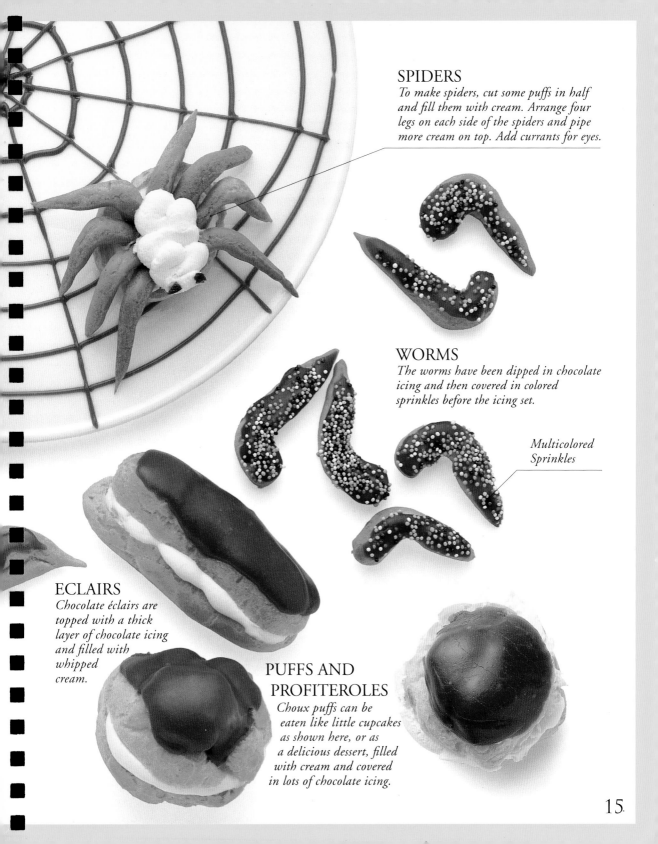

SPIDERS

To make spiders, cut some puffs in half and fill them with cream. Arrange four legs on each side of the spiders and pipe more cream on top. Add currants for eyes.

WORMS

The worms have been dipped in chocolate icing and then covered in colored sprinkles before the icing set.

Multicolored Sprinkles

ECLAIRS

Chocolate éclairs are topped with a thick layer of chocolate icing and filled with whipped cream.

PUFFS AND PROFITEROLES

Choux puffs can be eaten like little cupcakes as shown here, or as a delicious dessert, filled with cream and covered in lots of chocolate icing.

15

SWEET AND SAVORY SCONES

Here you can find out how to make sweet scones, fruit scones, and cheese scones. The ingredients shown will make about ten scones. Below you can see how to make sweet, fruit, and cheese scone doughs. Turn the page to find out how to cut out and fill your scones.

4 fl oz (120 ml) milk

You will need

½ cup (50 g) golden raisins

½ cup (50 g) grated cheddar cheese

MAKING SCONE DOUGH

Set the oven to 425°F/220°C. Put the flour and salt in the mixing bowl. Add the butter and cut it into pieces.

Rub the butter and flour together with your fingertips until the mixture looks like breadcrumbs. Stir in the sugar.

Add the milk to the mixture and stir everything together with the wooden spoon to make a smooth mixture.

16

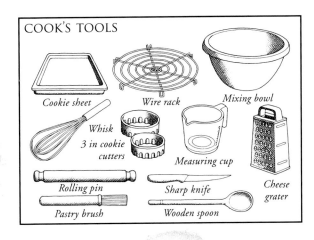

COOK'S TOOLS

Cookie sheet   Wire rack   Mixing bowl

Whisk
3 in cookie
cutters   Measuring cup   Cheese
grater

Rolling pin   Sharp knife

Pastry brush   Wooden spoon

*1½ cups (225 g)
self-rising flour*

*2 Tbsp (25 g)
fine sugar*

A pinch of salt

4 Tbsp (50 g) softened butter

Fruit scones

Cheese scones

Knead the mixture by pressing and squeezing it together with your hands until you have formed a stiff dough.

Follow the recipe for sweet scones but add the golden raisins to the mixture after you have stirred in the sugar.

Follow the same recipe for sweet scones, but add the grated cheese instead of the fine sugar before you add the milk.

17

TEATIME TREATS

You can use different shaped cookie cutters to make small scones, or make a big scone round with your hands. Scones taste best when warm, with or without butter. Try filling sweet or fruit scones with jam and whipped cream.

COOK'S TOOLS

Small bowl

Whisk

Sharp knife

Knife

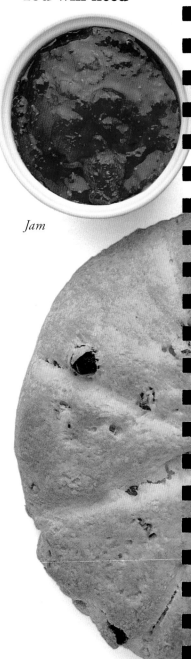

Jam

CUTTING OUT THE SCONES

Grease a cookie sheet. Gently roll out the dough until it is 1 in (2.5 cm) thick. Cut shapes with cookie cutters dipped in flour.

Put the scones on a cookie sheet*, brush them with milk and bake for 12 to 15 minutes, until firm and risen. Cool them on a wire rack.

A scone round

Roll the dough into a circle about 1 in (2.5 cm) thick. Divide the top into eight; brush it with milk. Bake for about 25 minutes.

Whipping the cream

Whisk the cream in the small bowl until it is thick. Cut the sweet or fruit scones in half and fill them with jam and cream.

18

Sprinkle some extra grated cheese on top of the cheese scones.

½ cup (150 ml)
heavy cream

Sweet scones

Strawberry jam

Whipped cream

Cheese scones

A fruit scone round

Grated cheddar cheese
sprinkled on before baking

FRUITY BREAD

A holiday wreath not only tastes good; it looks really festive too! Here you can see all you need to make a fruity bread wreath. The wreath will rise more quickly if you put it in an oiled plastic bag and then leave it in a warm place. Turn the page to see how to make the icing and marzipan for your wreath.

You will need

3 fl oz (75 ml) warm milk

2 Tbsp (25 g) butter

1 small egg

½ teaspoon salt

2 Tbsp (25 g) brown sugar

1½ cups (225 g) flour

Set oven to 400°F/200°C. Put the sugar, flour, yeast, salt, spice, and cinnamon in the bowl and stir together.

Add the butter and cut it up. Rub everything together with your fingertips until the mixture looks like fine breadcrumbs.

Add the fruit, egg, and milk. Mix them together to make a ball of dough. Knead the dough on a floured surface for five minutes.

20

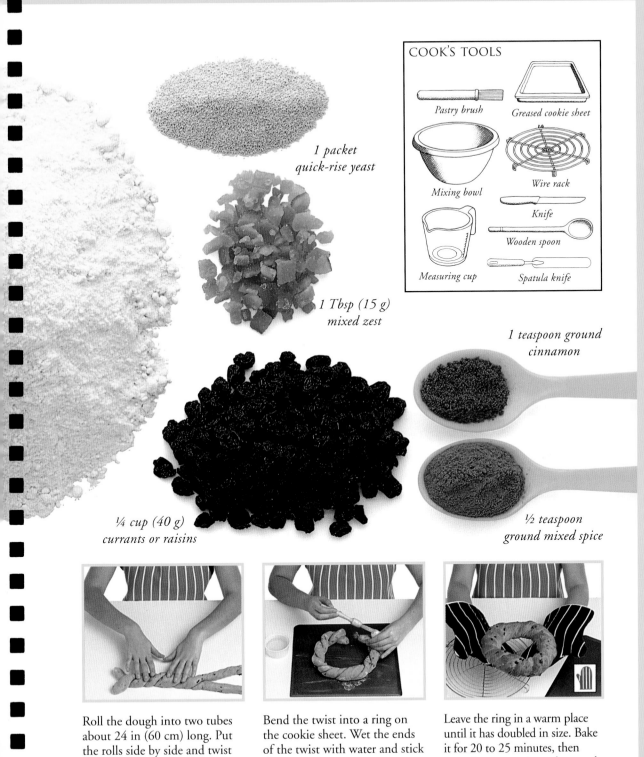

1 packet
quick-rise yeast

1 Tbsp (15 g)
mixed zest

1 teaspoon ground
cinnamon

¼ cup (40 g)
currants or raisins

½ teaspoon
ground mixed spice

COOK'S TOOLS

Pastry brush

Greased cookie sheet

Mixing bowl

Wire rack

Knife

Wooden spoon

Measuring cup

Spatula knife

Roll the dough into two tubes about 24 in (60 cm) long. Put the rolls side by side and twist them together.

Bend the twist into a ring on the cookie sheet. Wet the ends of the twist with water and stick them together.

Leave the ring in a warm place until it has doubled in size. Bake it for 20 to 25 minutes, then move it on to a wire rack to cool.

21

A HOLIDAY WREATH

Turn your fruity wreath into a holiday treat with a tangy lemon icing and some marzipan leaves and berries. You can use ready-made marzipan, or you can follow the recipe for fondant icing (see page 30).

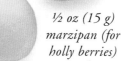

1 oz (25 g) marzipan (for holly leaves)

½ oz (15 g) marzipan (for holly berries)

1 tablespoon lemon juice

You will need

12 drops of green food coloring

12 drops of red food coloring

1 cup (175 g) powdered sugar

Coloring marzipan

Make a hole with your finger in the marzipan and add the food coloring. Knead the marzipan until it is an even color.

Holly leaves

Roll the green marzipan out on a sugared surface until it is thin and even. Cut out leaves with the cutter (or a knife).

Holly berries

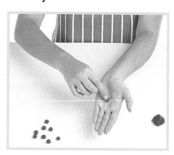

Take small pieces of red marzipan and roll them into balls with your fingers. Try to keep all the balls the same size.

MAKING ICING

COOK'S TOOLS

Sieve

Small bowl

Small holly leaf cutters*

Rolling pin

Wooden spoon

Sift the powdered sugar into the small bowl. Add the lemon juice and stir with the wooden spoon until the icing is smooth.

Spoon the icing along the top of the wreath and let it drip down the sides. Decorate the wreath before the icing sets.

The finished holiday wreath

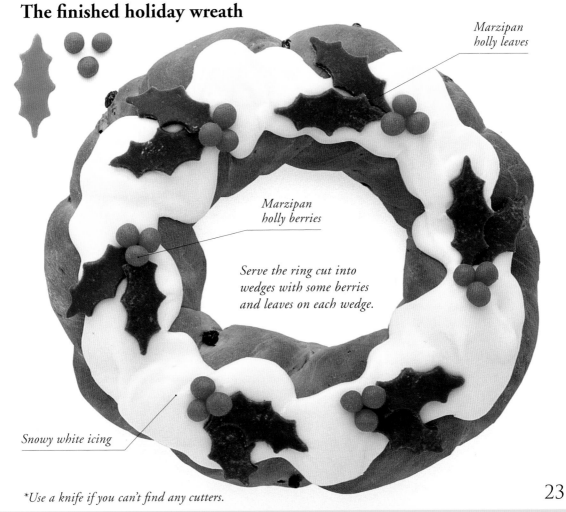

Marzipan holly leaves

Marzipan holly berries

Serve the ring cut into wedges with some berries and leaves on each wedge.

Snowy white icing

Use a knife if you can't find any cutters.

23

MAKING MERINGUES

Meringues are deliciously sweet and crunchy and are made from only the whites of eggs, some sugar, and a little salt. Separating the egg white from the yolk is a little tricky because yolks break very easily, so always start with more eggs than you need! Be very careful not to allow any yolk to mix with the egg whites, or the recipe won't work. Meringues take five hours to cook because they have to be baked in a cool oven to keep them white.

COOK'S TOOLS

Cookie sheet Large cup Cup Mixing bowl

Baking parchment Teaspoon Spatula knife

Tablespoon Whisk

Small bowl Sharp knife Scissors

You will need

A pinch of salt

2 eggs

Candied cherries

Currants

½ cup (100 g) fine sugar

Candied orange zest

24

WHAT TO DO

1. Set oven at its lowest setting. Cut out a square of parchment the same size as the cookie sheet. Put it on top of the cookie sheet.

2. *Crack one egg in half and pour the yolk from one half of the shell into the other, letting the egg white fall into the cup.

3. Pour the yolk into the cup and the white into the small bowl. Do the same thing again to separate the second egg.

Nests

4. Add a pinch of salt to the egg whites in the small bowl. Beat the egg whites with the whisk until they form stiff peaks.

5. Whisk the sugar into the egg whites a little at a time, until you have used all the sugar and the meringue looks glossy.

Shape a heaped tablespoonful of meringue into a circle on the cookie sheet. Make a hollow in the middle with a teaspoon.

Ghosts

Snowmen

Spread tablespoonfuls of meringue into ghost shapes with a teaspoon. Cut pieces of candied cherry to make eyes.

Use a teaspoonful of meringue for the head and a tablespoonful for the body. Decorate with pieces of currant, zest, and cherry.

Bake the meringue ghosts, snowmen, and nests slowly for four to five hours until firm. Put them on a wire rack to cool.

Ask an adult to help you with this.

25

SNOW-WHITE SURPRISES

Meringue nests make mouthwatering desserts when they are filled with cream and fruit. Use soft fruits and arrange them in patterns on the cream-filled nests. You could make nests at Easter and fill them with chocolate eggs, or make ghosts for a Halloween treat. Snowmen are lots of fun as Christmas decorations that you can eat !

Candied cherries

Mandarin segments

Seedless red and green grapes

Strawberries

Peach chunks

You will need

4 fl oz (120 ml) heavy cream

FILLING THE NESTS

Pour the cream into a small bowl. Whisk the cream until it is thick and fluffy and forms soft peaks.

Cut off all the strawberry stalks. Slice some of the strawberries and cut others into quarters with a sharp knife*.

Spoon the whipped cream into the nests and arrange the pieces of fruit in pretty patterns on top of them.

Ask an adult to help you.

The finished meringues

Meringue nests

Slice of strawberry

Piece of strawberry

Pieces of candied cherry for eyes

Ghosts

Peach chunk

Black grape

Mandarin segment

Whipped cream

Candied cherry

Green grape

Snowmen

Nose made from a triangle of candied zest

Candied cherry for a mouth

Currant eyes

Currant buttons

27

LITTLE CUPCAKES **You will need**

Sponge cupcakes are simple and quick to make. Here you can see everything you will need to make about ten small and ten tiny plain or cherry cupcakes. If you want to make more, you will have to double or triple the amounts of ingredients shown. Don't forget that you will need more icing too! On the next four pages there are lots of exciting ideas for icing and decorating all your cupcakes.

2 eggs

6 candied cherries

8 Tbsp (100 g) soft margarine

½ cup (100 g) fine sugar

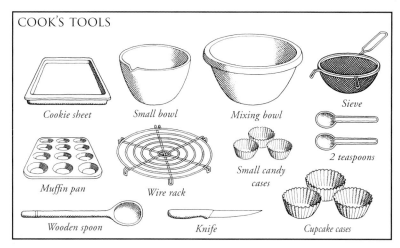

COOK'S TOOLS

Cookie sheet   *Small bowl*   *Mixing bowl*   *Sieve*

Muffin pan   *Wire rack*   *Small candy cases*   *2 teaspoons*

Wooden spoon   *Knife*   *Cupcake cases*

WHAT TO DO

1. Set the oven to 350°F/180°C. Put the larger paper cups in the pan and the candy cups on the cookie sheet.

2. Sieve the self-rising flour into the mixing bowl. Add the soft margarine and the fine sugar to the flour.

3. Break the eggs into the bowl. Beat everything together with the wooden spoon until the mixture is soft and creamy.

4. To make cherry cupcakes, cut the candied cherries into small pieces with a sharp knife* and stir them into the mixture.

5. Put two teaspoonfuls of the mixture into each larger paper cup and one teaspoonful into each candy cup.

6. Bake the tiny cupcakes for 10 to 15 minutes and the small ones for 20 to 25 minutes. Then put them on a wire rack to cool.

1 cup (100 g) self-rising flour

Ask an adult to help you.

29

ICING THE CUPCAKES

You can make lots of different icing for your cupcakes. Here you can find out how to make chocolate, white, and pink butter icing and how to color fondant icing and mold it into shapes. Look on the next two pages for lots of decorating ideas.

You will need

8 Tbsp (100 g) soft butter

8 Tbsp (100 g) ready-made fondant icing

2 tablespoons cocoa powder

3 drops red food coloring

1 cup (215 g) icing sugar

COOK'S TOOLS

Mixing bowl   Small bowl

Wooden spoon

Sharp knife

Sieve   Knife

WHAT TO DO

1. Put half the butter into the mixing bowl and cut it into small pieces. Beat it with the wooden spoon until it is creamy.

2. Shift two-thirds of the powdered sugar into a bowl. Mix the sugar into the butter a little at a time until the icing is creamy.

3. Divide the icing in half. Put half of it in a small bowl. Beat the red food coloring into the other half to make pink icing.

FONDANT ICING

4. To make chocolate icing, use the remainder of the powdered sugar and the cocoa power and follow steps 1 and 2 above.

To make pink fondant icing, add 3 drops of red food coloring to the fondant. Knead it until the color is even.

Make a roll of fondant for the elephant's trunk and shape flat circles for its ears. Make pig's ears from flat ovals of fondant.

CAKES WITH FACES

Remove the cupcakes from their cases. Arrange the small and tiny cupcakes together to make faces with ears or noses or both.

Ice the bottom and sides of a tiny cupcake and stick it on top of a small cupcake covered with the same colored icing.

When you have iced all your cupcakes, give them faces by decorating them with candy and chocolates before the icing dries.

31

FUNNY FACES

Cupcakes are lots of fun to make and they look really bright and colorful as well. Look out for all kinds of different chocolates and candy to use for decoration. Copy the butterflies, soldier, teddy bear, elephant, and other funny-face cupcakes shown here, or experiment with some ideas of your own! Why not try making funny-face cupcakes that look like your family and pets for a special family party.

You will need

Red liquorice strings

Liquorice pieces

Liquorice strips

White chocolate drops

Chocolate drops

Cherries

White chocolate buttons

Chocolate buttons

Sugar-coated candy

Chocolate sprinkles

Cherry cupcakes

Eat your cherry cupcakes as they are, or iced and decorated with candy.

Pink butter icing

Butterflies
Butter icing

Sponge wings

Pieces of candied cherry

Cut a circle out of some cupcakes and then cut the circles in half to make wings. Fill the hole in the cupcakes with butter or fondant icing and put a wing on each side.

32

PIG

Pink butter icing

Chocolate drop

TEDDY BEAR

Chocolate button

Chocolate sprinkles

RACOON

Chocolate sprinkles

SEAL

DOG

Chocolate drop

Liquorice

Liquorice on white chocolate button

Liquorice

Chocolate sprinkles

Pink fondant circles on tiny cakes for ears

SOLDIER

Red liquorice

ELEPHANT

Chocolate sprinkle-covered cupcake

Liquorice

Pink fondant curled up on a tiny cupcake

33

A RICH CHOCOLATE CAKE

No birthday or party is complete without a surprise cake—so here's how to make a wonderful chocolate cake that tastes delicious. Look on the next two pages for different ways of decorating the cake with sifted powdered sugar, or with yummy candy.

You will need

8 Tbsp (100 g) softened butter

8 fl oz (250 ml) milk

2 large eggs

1 tablespoon lemon juice

COOK'S TOOLS

Wire rack

Wax paper   Mixing bowl

Pencil   Greased 9 in-deep cake pan

Scissors   Measuring cup

Dessert spoon

Sieve   Wooden spoon

WHAT TO DO

Set the oven to 350°F/180°C. Draw around the cake pan on wax paper. Cut out the circle and put it in the pan.

Stir the lemon juice into the milk. Put the butter and half the sugar into the mixing bowl and heat it until pale and fluffy.

34

1 cup (250 g)
fine sugar

1 teaspoon baking soda

3 Tbsp (50 g)
cocoa powder

2 cups (225 g) all-purpose flour

Beat the eggs into the mixture
one at a time. Stir in the rest of
the sugar. Sift the flour, soda,
and cocoa powder together.

Beat in half the milk and fold in
half the flour. Add the rest of
the milk and then the rest of the
flour. Mix until smooth.

Pour the mixture into the cake
pan and bake it for one hour.
Then tip the cake out of the pan
and put it on a wire rack to cool.

DECORATED CAKES

Here are two ways to decorate your cake. Both cakes use the stencils found at the back of the book. Turn to pages 30 to 31 to find out how to make the chocolate frosting for the cake shown opposite.

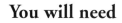

You will need

Powdered sugar in a fine-meshed sieve

Using the star stencil

Tear the star stencil out of the back of the book. Place the stencil on top of the cake then gently sift powdered sugar over the top. Remove the stencil.

Tap the sieve so the sugar reaches the corners of the star.

36

You will need

Red liquorice

Colored sprinkles

Jelly beans

Sugar-coated candy

Colorful sugar-coated candies form a pattern

Pour multicolored sprinkles through the balloon stencil found at the back of the book.

Red liquorice balloon strings

Row of jelly beans

HEALTHY MUFFINS

Muffins are really easy and quick and make
a delicious breakfast treat. This recipe makes
12 scrumptious blueberry muffins. If you
like, you can use raspberries, cherries
(pitted and chopped), chopped-up apricots,
or even chocolate chips instead of the
blueberries. Just add them at step 3.

You will need

2 cups (250 g) self-rising flour

½ teaspoon
vanilla
extract

½ cup (140 g) golden fine sugar

5 fl oz (150 ml) milk

1 large egg

4 fl oz (120 ml)
vegetable oil

6 oz (175 g)
fresh blueberries

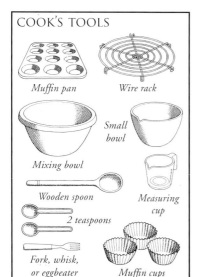

COOK'S TOOLS

Muffin pan   Wire rack

Small
bowl

Mixing bowl

Wooden spoon   Measuring
cup

2 teaspoons

Fork, whisk,
or eggbeater   Muffin cups

WHAT TO DO

1. Ask an adult to help you. Set the oven to 400°F/200°C. Put the muffin cups in the muffin pan and set to one side.

2. Crack the egg in a bowl. Beat it slightly with a fork or a whisk, then mix in the milk, vanilla extract, and oil.

3. Mix the flour and sugar in another bowl. Scoop a well in the middle, then add the blueberries and pour in the wet ingredients.

4. Fold the mixture together gently in a few strokes with a wooden spoon. It does not matter if the mixture looks lumpy.

5. Spoon the mixture into the muffin cups so each one is half full, then bake for 20–25 minutes until golden brown.

Leave the muffins to cool on a wire rack

The finished muffins

39

PEANUT BUTTER COOKIES

These mouthwatering cookies are very quick and easy to make. Crunchy peanut butter makes the cookies very nutty, but use smooth peanut butter if you prefer it. Bake the cookies for 15 minutes if you like them soft in the middle, or for 20 to 25 minutes if you like them crisp. Store the cookies in an airtight container to keep them fresh.

You will need

4 oz (125 g) crunchy peanut butter

1 egg

1 cup (175 g) soft brown sugar

COOK'S TOOLS

2 teaspoons

Wooden spoon

Mixing bowl

Wire rack

Knife

Greased cookie sheet

8 Tbsp (125 g) soft butter

1¼ cup (175 g) self-rising flour

40

WHAT TO DO

Set the oven to 350°F/180°C. Cut up the butter in the bowl and add the sugar. Beat them together until fluffy.

Add the peanut butter, flour, and egg and beat everything together with the wooden spoon until the mixture is smooth.

Put teaspoonfuls of mixture on to a cookie sheet. Bake the cookies for 15 to 25 minutes*. Then put them on a wire rack to cool.

The finished cookies

*See the introduction to this recipe.

41

SIMPLE SHORTBREAD

Two-tone shortbread cookies are lots of fun to make and eat. On this page, you can see everything you will need to make plain and chocolate shortbread dough. The ingredients shown below make enough shortbread for eight owl's eyes, eight lollipops, and twelve window cookies. Look on the next page to find out how to make each cookie and to see the finished results.

For plain shortbread

8 Tbsp (125 g) softened butter

COOK'S TOOLS

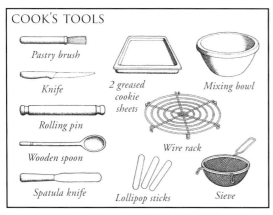

Pastry brush

Knife

2 greased cookie sheets

Mixing bowl

Rolling pin

Wire rack

Wooden spoon

Spatula knife

Lollipop sticks

Sieve

You will need

¼ cup (50 g) fine sugar

1 Tbsp (15 g) cocoa powder

8 almonds

1¼ cup (175 g) all-purpose flour

For chocolate shortbread

8 Tbsp (125 g) softened butter

¼ cup (50 g) fine sugar

3 tablespoons milk

*1 cup (160 g)
all-purpose flour*

MAKING PLAIN SHORTBREAD

1. Set the oven to 350°F/180°C. Sift flour into the mixing bowl. Stir in the fine sugar.

2. Add butter, cut up. Rub the flour, sugar, and butter together with your fingers until the mixture is like breadcrumbs.

3. Add a tablespoonful of milk to the mixture. Mix everything together with your hands to form a ball of dough.

MAKING CHOCOLATE SHORTBREAD

Sift flour and the cocoa powder together. Make the chocolate dough in the same way as the plain dough.

Divide each ball of dough into three equal pieces. You will need one plain and one chocolate piece to make each type of shortbread.

43

COOKIE BAZAAR

OWL'S EYES

Roll a piece of each type of dough into a square 6 in by 6 in (15 cm by 15 cm). Brush the top of each square with milk.

Put the square on top of another and roll them up together. Then cut the roll into 16 slices, as shown.

Stick two slices together with milk to make each cookie. Put the cookie on a cookie sheet. Add an almond beak to each one.

LOLLIPOPS

Roll out the chocolate dough into a square 4 in by 4 in (10 cm by 10 cm). Make the plain dough into a roll 4 in (10 cm) long.

Brush the chocolate square with milk and wrap it around the plain roll. Squeeze the ends of the chocolate dough together.

Cut the roll into eight slices. Put the slices on to the cookie sheet and push a lollipop stick into the middle of each one.

WINDOWS

Shape the two kinds of dough into rectangles (4 cm by 9 cm) with your hands. Cut them in half lengthwise.

Stick two strips of plain and chocolate dough together with milk. Stick the other two strips on top of them, as shown.

Cut the block of dough strips into 12 square slices with a sharp knife. Put the slices on to a cookie sheet.

Baking the cookies

Bake the cookies in the top half of the oven for 15 to 20 minutes, until they are a pale gold color. The lollipop cookies are thicker and will take slightly longer to cook. When the cookies are done, carefully move them from the cookie sheets and put on a wire rack to cool and harden.

Storing cookies

Cookies become soggy if they are left out for too long. Store them in an airtight container to keep them fresh and crunchy.

The finished cookies

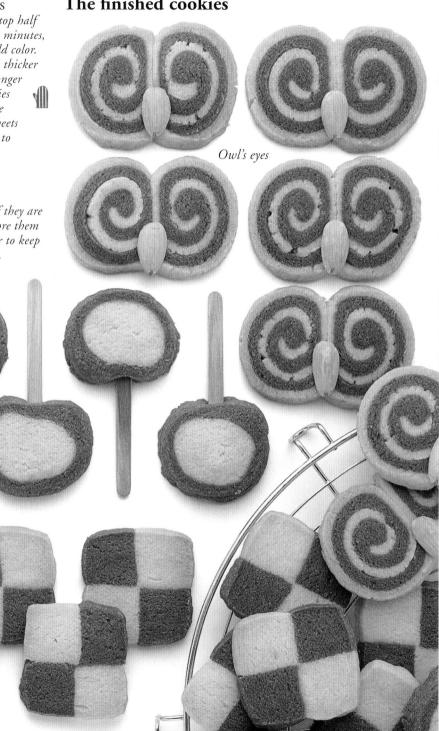

Owl's eyes

Lollipops

Windows

CHOCOLATE BROWNIES

Chocolate brownies are crisp on the outside, but wonderfully soft and chewy inside. Below are all the ingredients you need to make dark chocolate and walnut brownies. On the next page you will find the finished brownie squares.

COOK'S TOOLS

Shallow baking pan

Wire rack

Saucepan

Mixing bowl

Small bowl

Scissors

Fork

Wax paper

Wooden spoon

Knife

You will need

1 cup (175 g) soft brown sugar

5 Tbsp (65 g) butter

2 oz (50 g) unsweetened chocolate

WHAT TO DO

Set the oven to 350°F/180°C. Cut a square of wax paper and put it in the bottom of the greased baking pan.

Heat some water in the saucepan until it just starts to bubble. Put the butter in the small bowl and cut it up.

Break up the chocolate into the bowl and stand it over the pan. Stir the butter and chocolate together until they have melted.

½ cup (65 g)
walnut pieces

2 eggs

½ cup (65 g)
self-rising flour

Break the eggs into the mixing bowl and beat with a fork. Add the flour, walnuts, and sugar and mix with the wooden spoon.

Pour the melted chocolate and butter into the mixture in the bowl and beat hard until the mixture is smooth.

Pour the mixture into the baking pan and bake for 30 to 35 minutes. Leave it to cool and then cut it into squares.

47

A BROWNIE PACK

Brownies can be made with any
kind of chocolate or nut. Try using
white or milk chocolate instead of
unsweetened chocolate and using
other kinds of nut, such as
hazelnuts, peanuts, or almonds
instead of walnuts.

The finished brownies